TEN QUESTIONS

John Hegar[t]

Mental Maths

The first two Mental Maths books were all about the number bonds up to twenty – that is, the basic facts such as **2 + 6 = 8**. These facts have to be learnt, and those books included many opportunities for your child to learn, remember and use them with growing confidence by answering questions and playing simple games.

This book uses the same number bonds to practise adding and taking away of numbers up to fifty. New ideas are presented in ways that point out the patterns in numbers, making links with what has already been learnt. For example, if you know that **2 + 6 = 8**, and that **12 + 6 = 18**, it should be easy to see that **22 + 6 = 28**, **32 + 6 = 38**, and so on. Children can't always explain these patterns, but if they can understand them intuitively and use them successfully the explanations can come later.

Introduced in this book is the idea that your child should start learning ways of checking results without needing you or a teacher to do it for them. The ability to do this is a key step towards developing the confidence to work independently, and it will become more important as Mental Maths progresses.

Ages 8–9

Letts

TEN QUESTIONS A DAY

Mixed take-away

15 – 11 = 4

13 – 6 = 7

14 – 3 = 11

12 – 7 = 5

11 – 8 = 3

14 – 6 = 8

15 – 9 = 6

13 – 0 = 13

11 – 6 = 5

12 – 3 = 9

Helper's tips

- Say 'Fifteen take away eleven leaves ...'
- These questions revise the number bonds up to fifteen which were covered in the first two Mental Maths books.

Mixed take-away

16 – 12 = 4

13 – 5 = 8

18 – 7 = 11

17 – 14 = 3

19 – 7 = 12

15 – 3 = 12

18 – 14 = 4

16 – 9 = 7

17 – 12 = 5

19 – 3 = 16

Helper's tips

- The number bonds up to twenty were covered in the previous book. Go back over those pages if your child is not sure of them.
- Make a set of twenty cards, each showing one number from one to twenty. Shuffle the cards and lay them out face down in four rows of five. Ask your child to turn over any two cards. If the numbers on the cards add up to twenty they keep the cards, if not they turn them back over. Continue until all the bonds for twenty have been made. Which two cards will always be left over?

Mixed take-away

14 – 2 = 12

20 – 7 = 13

18 – 11 = 7

16 – 1 = 15

20 – 18 = 2

18 – 6 = 12

20 – 9 = 11

19 – 5 = 14

17 – 15 = 2

20 – 6 = 14

Helper's tip

Taking away can always be done by adding: '14 is 2 add how many ...?'

Mixed take-away

18 – 5 = 13

20 – 14 = 6

17 – 8 = 9

19 – 11 = 8

20 – 3 = 17

16 – 8 = 8

19 – 12 = 7

18 – 2 = 16

17 – 11 = 6

19 – 16 = 3

Helper's tip

Play number-bond bingo.

- Make players' cards containing numbers up to twenty.
- Call out a two-number sum such as '18 – 7', '15 – 3' and so on.
- The players have to cross off the correct answers to the sums.

Mixed adding and taking away

6 + 6 = 12

12 – 6 = 6

15 – 8 = 7

8 + 7 = 15

15 – 7 = 8

6 + 3 = 9

9 – 6 = 3

8 + 9 = 17

17 – 8 = 9

17 – 9 = 8

Helper's tips

- Read these quite slowly and clearly to give your child a chance to hear the 'add' or 'take away' instruction.
- The same number bond can be written in up to four different ways. Make sure your child notices this.

Mixed adding and taking away

19 – 9 = 10

10 + 9 = 19

19 – 10 = 9

8 – 6 = 2

2 + 6 = 8

15 – 10 = 5

5 + 10 = 15

15 – 5 = 10

11 – 6 = 5

11 – 5 = 6

Helper's tip

If you take a number away then add it back, or if you add a number then take it away, you end up where you started. This simple fact allows us to check the result of any addition or subtraction. You check addition by taking away again and subtraction by adding back.

Mixed adding and taking away

13 + 5 = 18

18 – 5 = 13

15 + 3 = 18

18 – 15 = 3

18 – 3 = 15

16 + 4 = 20

14 + 6 = 20

20 – 16 = 4

20 – 14 = 6

20 – 6 = 14

Helper's tip

Because our number system is based on ten, the first five questions are really about 3 + 5 = 8 and add another 10 to make 18. At this stage, your child can notice the pattern and use it without needing to understand why it works.

Adding three numbers

2 + 3 + 6 = 11

5 + 7 + 4 = 16

6 + 6 + 3 = 15

8 + 7 + 5 = 20

4 + 9 + 3 = 16

5 + 8 + 6 = 19

7 + 2 + 3 = 12

6 + 9 + 4 = 19

9 + 5 + 3 = 17

8 + 1 + 6 = 15

Helper's tip

Say 'Two add three ... add six makes ...?' (Your child can add the numbers in any order.)

Adding, then taking away

$5 + 5 - 3 = 7$

$10 + 7 - 4 = 13$

$6 + 9 - 5 = 10$

$8 + 10 - 6 = 12$

$9 + 9 - 2 = 16$

$5 + 10 - 1 = 14$

$9 + 8 - 4 = 13$

$7 + 6 - 9 = 4$

$8 + 6 - 5 = 9$

$7 + 7 - 3 = 11$

Helper's tips

- Say 'Five add five ... take away three makes ...?'
- Make sure your child understands that the order cannot be reversed when taking away. For example, 5 – 3 does not produce the same result as 3 – 5.

Adding, then taking away

8 + 7 – 2 = 13

6 + 10 – 8 = 8

5 + 7 – 1 = 11

9 + 5 – 4 = 10

8 + 8 – 1 = 15

9 + 7 – 5 = 11

6 + 6 – 3 = 9

10 + 9 – 7 = 12

5 + 8 – 4 = 9

4 + 10 – 7 = 7

Helper's tip

Draw a ladder and number the rungs from one to twenty. Put a counter or coin at the foot of the ladder and move it on the throw of two dice: the first tells you the number of rungs to climb up, the second the number of rungs to climb down. The objective is to land on twenty. If you go off the top or the bottom of the ladder, start again.

Change from 20 pence

20 pence – 8 pence = 12 pence

20 pence – 14 pence = 6 pence

20 pence – 5 pence = 15 pence

20 pence – 16 pence = 4 pence

20 pence – 11 pence = 9 pence

20 pence – 3 pence = 17 pence

20 pence – 18 pence = 2 pence

20 pence – 10 pence = 10 pence

20 pence – 6 pence = 14 pence

20 pence – 1 penny = 19 pence

Helper's tip

Say 'How much is left from twenty pence if I spend eight pence?'

Change from 20 pence

20 pence – 7 pence = 13 pence

20 pence – 15 pence = 5 pence

20 pence – 9 pence = 11 pence

20 pence – 12 pence = 8 pence

20 pence – 10 pence = 10 pence

20 pence – 13 pence = 7 pence

20 pence – 2 pence = 18 pence

20 pence – 17 pence = 3 pence

20 pence – 4 pence = 16 pence

20 pence – 19 pence = 1 penny

Helper's tip

Ask your child to investigate this question on paper. If you have one of each denomination of British coin from a penny to a twenty-pence piece, how many different amounts can you make? (e.g. 1p, 2p: 1p + 2p = 3p, and so on)

Adding ten

$8 + 10 = 18$

$13 + 10 = 23$

$19 + 10 = 29$

$10 + 10 = 20$

$15 + 10 = 25$

$10 + 16 = 26$

$10 + 12 = 22$

$17 + 10 = 27$

$10 + 11 = 21$

$14 + 10 = 24$

Helper's tips

- Adding ten just means adding one to the figure in the tens column.
- For extra practice read out the answers to these questions and ask your child to add another ten to each of them.

Adding twenty

20 + 10 = 30

20 + 11 = 31

20 + 12 = 32

13 + 20 = 33

14 + 20 = 34

20 + 15 = 35

16 + 20 = 36

20 + 17 = 37

18 + 20 = 38

20 + 19 = 39

Helper's tips

- This time we are adding two to the figure in the tens column, because twenty means two tens.
- For extra practice read out the answers to these questions and ask your child to add another ten to each of them.

Adding nine

16 + 9 = 25

24 + 9 = 33

18 + 9 = 27

22 + 9 = 31

17 + 9 = 26

19 + 9 = 28

25 + 9 = 34

13 + 9 = 22

21 + 9 = 30

20 + 9 = 29

Helper's tip

A good way of adding nine is to add ten and take away one. Suggest this to your child before you begin this page.

Adding eight

28 + 8 = 36

17 + 8 = 25

39 + 8 = 47

32 + 8 = 40

23 + 8 = 31

36 + 8 = 44

34 + 8 = 42

40 + 8 = 48

31 + 8 = 39

35 + 8 = 43

Helper's tip

Following the pattern of the last two pages, can your child suggest a similar way of adding eight? (Add ten and take away two.)

Mixed adding

5 + 14 = 19

7 + 13 = 20

2 + 15 = 17

8 + 16 = 24

4 + 12 = 16

2 + 19 = 21

5 + 17 = 22

6 + 14 = 20

2 + 13 = 15

4 + 18 = 22

Helper's tip

5 + 14 is the same as 5 + 4 + 10. Make sure your child understands that each two-figure number in these questions breaks up into tens and units in this way.

Mixed adding

7 + 14 = 21

5 + 13 = 18

6 + 16 = 22

5 + 19 = 24

7 + 12 = 19

5 + 16 = 21

3 + 14 = 17

8 + 17 = 25

6 + 13 = 19

8 + 19 = 27

Helper's tip

Saying 'Seven add four–teen' can make it easier for your child to hear that this is the same as 7 + 4 + 10.

Mixed adding

22 + 8 = 30

39 + 4 = 43

26 + 7 = 33

15 + 5 = 20

38 + 3 = 41

27 + 7 = 34

16 + 2 = 18

44 + 4 = 48

29 + 6 = 35

38 + 8 = 46

Helper's tip

22 + 8 breaks up into 20 + 2 + 8. Remember, changing the order makes no difference when adding. Your child might prefer to turn it into 8 + 20 + 2.

Mixed adding

33 + 3 = 36

18 + 5 = 23

29 + 9 = 38

42 + 2 = 44

37 + 9 = 46

39 + 3 = 42

46 + 4 = 50

25 + 7 = 32

13 + 8 = 21

37 + 3 = 40

Helper's tip

Keep revising the number bonds so that your child will be ready for adding tens and units in the next book.

Take away ten

23 – 10 = 13

28 – 10 = 18

34 – 10 = 24

40 – 10 = 30

37 – 10 = 27

26 – 10 = 16

42 – 10 = 32

39 – 10 = 29

45 – 10 = 35

21 – 10 = 11

Helper's tip

Just take away one from the tens column.

Take away nine

16 – 9 = 7

24 – 9 = 15

18 – 9 = 9

32 – 9 = 23

37 – 9 = 28

29 – 9 = 20

45 – 9 = 36

13 – 9 = 4

31 – 9 = 22

50 – 9 = 41

Helper's tip

Take away ten, then add one.

Take away nine

28 – 9 = 19

17 – 9 = 8

39 – 9 = 30

22 – 9 = 13

43 – 9 = 34

36 – 9 = 27

34 – 9 = 25

40 – 9 = 31

21 – 9 = 12

44 – 9 = 35

Helper's tip

Add one, then take away ten.

Take away eight

28 – 8 = 20

17 – 8 = 9

39 – 8 = 31

22 – 8 = 14

43 – 8 = 35

36 – 8 = 28

34 – 8 = 26

40 – 8 = 32

21 – 8 = 13

45 – 8 = 37

Helper's tip

Take away ten and add two if your child finds it easier this way.

Mixed take-away

19 – 10 = 9

28 – 4 = 24

14 – 3 = 11

36 – 6 = 30

27 – 5 = 22

19 – 3 = 16

35 – 2 = 33

41 – 1 = 40

28 – 6 = 22

37 – 2 = 35

Helper's tips

- The tens figure stays the same in these questions. Only the units figure changes.
- Check your answers by adding back the number you took away. This should take you back to where you started. For example, 19 – 10 = 9; 9 + 10 = 19

Mixed take-away

16 – 4 = 12

25 – 3 = 22

19 – 5 = 14

28 – 7 = 21

17 – 4 = 13

29 – 4 = 25

18 – 7 = 11

46 – 2 = 44

19 – 6 = 13

28 – 1 = 27

Helper's tips

- Again only the units figure changes. Check answers by adding back.
- Don't go on if your child has problems with this page. Repeat the last two pages until your child can do them correctly.

Mixed take-away

17 – 8 = 9

24 – 6 = 18

13 – 8 = 5

21 – 7 = 14

28 – 9 = 19

16 – 9 = 7

25 – 8 = 17

24 – 9 = 15

23 – 7 = 16

38 – 9 = 29

Helper's tips

- Try doing these by adding on. For example, 17 – 8 becomes '8 add on how many to get to 17?'
- Use the short cuts (see pages 23–25) for taking away 9 and 8.

Mixed take-away

26 – 7 = 19

45 – 7 = 38

24 – 5 = 19

31 – 4 = 27

22 – 8 = 14

35 – 6 = 29

44 – 8 = 36

23 – 5 = 18

31 – 8 = 23

22 – 6 = 16

Helper's tip

For 26 – 7 you would say '7 add how many to reach 10?' (3); '10 add how many more to reach 26?' (16); 'how many altogether from 7 to 26?' (19, that is 3 + 16). This seems complicated at first but soon becomes easy with practice.

Mixed take-away

24 – 7 = 17

42 – 9 = 33

21 – 6 = 15

36 – 8 = 28

23 – 9 = 14

32 – 7 = 25

21 – 3 = 18

43 – 6 = 37

32 – 3 = 29

25 – 9 = 16

Helper's tips

- Working these out by adding on (as on the previous page) is the most practical way to do it mentally.
- Your child might still have problems doing this. Don't worry, there will be more practice in the next book.

Change from 50 pence

50 pence – 9 pence = 41 pence

50 pence – 7 pence = 43 pence

50 pence – 4 pence = 46 pence

50 pence – 8 pence = 42 pence

50 pence – 5 pence = 45 pence

50 pence – 1 penny = 49 pence

50 pence – 3 pence = 47 pence

50 pence – 6 pence = 44 pence

50 pence – 10 pence = 40 pence

50 pence – 2 pence = 48 pence

Helper's tip

Do these too by counting on. For 50 pence – 9 pence you would say '9 pence add how much to reach 10 pence?' (1p); '10 pence add how much more to reach 50 pence?' (40p); 'how much is added altogether?' (41p, that is 1p + 40p).

Change from 50 pence

50 pence – 11 pence = 39 pence

50 pence – 15 pence = 35 pence

50 pence – 18 pence = 32 pence

50 pence – 13 pence = 37 pence

50 pence – 20 pence = 30 pence

50 pence – 14 pence = 36 pence

50 pence – 17 pence = 33 pence

50 pence – 19 pence = 31 pence

50 pence – 12 pence = 38 pence

50 pence – 16 pence = 34 pence

Helper's tip

This time count on to reach 20 pence, and from there add another 30 pence to reach 50 pence.